S0-AXJ-283

Walt Disney's
DONALD DUCK ADVENTURES

TAKE-ALONG COMIC

GEMSTONE PUBLISHING
TIMONIUM, MARYLAND

STEPHEN A. GEPPI
President/Publisher and Chief Executive Officer

JOHN K. SNYDER JR.
Chief Administrative Officer

STAFF

LEONARD (JOHN) CLARK
Editor-in-Chief

GARY LEACH
Art Director

SUSAN DAIGLE-LEACH
Production Manager

MELISSA BOWERSOX
Production Assistant

• IN THIS ISSUE •

Original cover and interior color provided by **Egmont**

Color modifications by
Susan Daigle-Leach and **Gary Leach**

Lettering and additional dialogue by **Gary Leach**

ADVERTISING/ MARKETING

J.C. VAUGHN
Executive Editor
Toll Free
(888) 375-9800 Ext. 413
ads@gemstonepub.com

ARNOLD T. BLUMBERG
Editor

BRENDA BUSICK
Creative Director

JAMIE DAVID
Executive Liaison

SARA ORTT
Assistant Executive Liaison

MARK HUESMAN
Production Assistant

MIKE WILBUR
Shipping Manager

WALT DISNEY'S DONALD DUCK ADVENTURES 2
Take-Along Comic
September, 2003

Published monthly by
Gemstone Publishing

© 2003 Disney Enterprises, Inc., except where noted. All rights reserved.

Nothing contained herein may be reproduced without the written permission of Disney Enterprises, Inc., Burbank, CA., or other copyright holders. **Application to mail at periodical class postage rates is pending at West Plains, MO.** 12-issue subscription rates: In the U.S., $95.40. In Canada, $105.00, payable in U.S. funds. For advertising rates and information call (888) 375-9800 ext. 413. Subscription and advertising rates subject to change without notice. Postmaster: send address changes to Walt Disney's Donald Duck Adventures / Take-Along Comic, PO Box 469, West Plains, MO, 65775.

PRINTED IN CANADA

THIS TRIP'S BEEN A SERIES OF CALAMITIES!

RIGHT! A DIARY OF DISASTERS FROM THE WORD GO!

VOILA! A BATCH OF SPICY OATMEAL TO WARM OUR TUMMIES!

OH, RATS!

SNAP!

THEN AGAIN, IT NEVER HURTS TO ...UM...CUT DOWN ON CALORIES!

WHO CARES ABOUT OUR FIGURES?

NOW WE'RE COLD *AND* HUNGRY!

DON'T BLAME ME! THESE THINGS HAPPEN, Y'KNOW!

"THESE THINGS HAPPEN"! THE STORY OF THIS TRIP!

BOY, A FEW THINGS GO WRONG, AND YOU RUNTS PEG IT ON ME!

LOOK AROUND! THERE'S NO ONE ELSE HERE BUT US - YOUR VICTIMS!

LISTEN, YOU LITTLE MISFITS! GLADSTONE EXCEPTED, MY LUCK'S AS GOOD AS THE NEXT GUY'S! IN FACT, BETTER! YOU'RE JUST SORE 'CAUSE...

WHIZZ!

LOOK!

WHIZZ!

A METEOR!

AND IT'S HEADING THIS WAY!

HA! TELL ME YOU'RE NOT LUCKY TO SEE *THAT*!

BANG!

WOW!

AMAZING IT DIDN'T LAND ON US!

COME ON! LET'S GO SEE!

EH, RIGHT!

THAT METEOR MUST'VE WEAKENED THE ROOF!

SO WHICH WAY'S OUT?

HELLO! WHAT'S THIS?

AH! LIGHT AT LAST!

HUH! WE FELL INTO AN OLD MINE!

NIFTY!

CHECK THIS OUT, BOYS! I FOUND AN OLD VASE!

UNCA DONALD, THIS IS NO TIME FOR COLLECTING SOUVENIRS!

WE'VE GOT TO GET OUT OF HERE!

HELLO! YOU FOLKS SEE A METEOR LAND NEAR HERE?

YEAH! A BIG, ROUND, KNOBBY THING!

BE CAREFUL! IT'S OVER AN OLD MINE!

WITH A ROTTEN ROOF!

THANKS FOR THE UPDATE! GUESS I'LL UNLOAD AND WAIT FOR THE HEAVY GEAR!

WHAT DO YOU PLAN TO DO WITH IT?

TAKE IT TO THE GEOLOGY MUSEUM FOR TESTS! STRUCTURE, COMPOSITION, ORIGINS! EVEN ALIEN ORGANISMS!

ALIEN ORGANISMS?

ON A BIT OF OLD ROCK?

THE DIRECTOR AT THE SPACE CENTER IS A KEEN BELIEVER IN ALIENS!

WHAT'S GOING ON?

A WILD ANIMAL GOT INTO MY SHOULDER PACK! IT TRIED TO STRANGLE ME!

WHAT KIND OF ANIMAL?

NO IDEA! IT BOUNDED AWAY TOO FAST! BUT I'VE TRAPPED IT IN THE BASEMENT!

CLICK!

WATCH THAT DOOR! I'M GONNA CALL THE POLICE!

NUTS! NOW THE *PHONES* ARE OUT OF ORDER!

IT JUST KEEPS GETTING BETTER!

IT COULD BE WORSE! AT LEAST THAT CREATURE DIDN'T THROTTLED ME!

I'LL POP DOWN TO THE NEAREST PAY PHONE!

UNFORTU-NATELY...

SHEESH! I TRIED FIVE PAY PHONES, AND THEY'RE *ALL* OUT OF ORDER!

I'LL HAVE TO WALK TO THE POLICE STATION, BUT FIRST I'D BETTER CHECK ON...

YIKES! ITS ESCAPED!

KIDS! QUICK! ARM YOUR-SELVES! THAT MONSTER'S ON THE LOOSE!

WE KNOW!

WE BROUGHT IT UP FROM THE CELLAR AFTER WE CHECKED THE FUSES!

IT WAS DIRTY AND DISTRESSED, SO WE GAVE IT A BATH!

GASP!

IT'LL BE MORE THAN DISTRESSED WHEN I'M THROUGH! STAND BACK!

CALM DOWN, UNCA DONALD!

HE'S HARMLESS!

HARMLESS? THAT THING NEARLY TIED MY WINDPIPE IN A HALFHITCH!

HE WAS JUST SCARED!

HE LIKES BUBBLE BATHS, SO WE NAMED HIM SOAPY!

WE'RE NOT SURE, BUT WE THINK HE'S A BABY PLATYPUS!

JUST KEEP IT AWAY FROM ME!

DON'T BE SILLY! HE'S VERY GENTLE!

HERE! HOLD HIM!

UH! WHAT'S HE DOING?

JUST SHOWING HE LIKES YOU!

NUZZLE!

AND SO...

HI! I FOUND THIS STRANGE ANIMAL IN THE WOODS...

DUCKBURG ZOO

FINE! LEAVE IT WITH US! WE'LL TAKE CARE OF IT!

THE THING IS, WE'D LIKE TO KEEP HIM! AND HE MAY NOT BE WILD, BECAUSE HE WAS WEARING A...

LET ME GET HIM CHECKED OVER AND THEN WE'LL TALK ABOUT IT!

HE'S A FUNNY LITTLE THING, AND VERY SHY! BE GENTLE WITH HIM!

DON'T WORRY! WE TAKE GOOD CARE OF OUR ANIMALS!

DIRECTOR! I WAS JUST COMING TO FETCH YOU! THAT NEW PROF IS ACTING VERY STRANGE!

HOOOOOOOOWL!

LAB

CONTROL ROOM

AHH! JUST AS I THOUGHT!

SCREEEEEECH!

MY, MY! HOW VERY INTERESTING! WE MUST TAKE A CLOSER LOOK!

JUST THEN...

OK! YOU CAN POP BACK IN A HOUR!

BY THE WAY, HE WAS WEARING...

RUMBLE!

WHAT THE BLAZES...

WHAT'S GOING ON? THERE'S A RHINO LOOSE!

IT'S NOT JUST THE RHINO! ALL THE CAGE LOCKS HAVE FAILED!

RUMBLE!

THEN CALL THE FIRE DEPARTMENT! IT'LL TAKE HIGH-PRESSURE HOSES TO DRIVE THEM BACK!

ALREADY DONE! THEY'RE ON THEIR WAY!

ABOUT THIS...

EXCUSE ME! THIS IS AN EMERGENCY!

DREADED DRAGON BONES! THE GIZOID HAS SKIPPED!

SO HAS OUR BOUNTY MONEY, LESS WE FIND HIS HIDE PRONTO!

IT'S SMELL IS STRONG! IT CAN'T BE FAR AWAY!

GOOD! WE HAVE LITTLE TIME! THE POD'S DISTRESS SIGNAL IS STILL OPERATING!

I KNOW! WE HAVE TO FIND THAT GIZOID BEFORE A RESCUE MISSION ARRIVES, AS WELL AS TAKE CARE OF ANY EARTHLINGS WHO'VE BEEN IN CONTACT WITH HIM!

THE TRACKER WILL LIKELY LAND WHERE THE POD DID! MAYBE WE CAN MEET IT AND NEUTRALIZE IT!

PERHAPS! BUT FIRST LET'S CHECK OUR SCANNER FOR A GIZOID SIGNAL!

THE GIZOID'S WRATH SHIELD MAY BE UP, HIDING IT FROM DETECTION!

NO, I HAVE A SIGNAL!

BEEP!

MY METEORITE!

WHAT HAVE YOU DONE TO IT?

IT WASN'T ME! IT WAS A PAIR OF BIG, UGLY ALIEN BEETLES!

THEY'RE ARMED AND HUNTING LITTLE SOAPY, WHO ISN'T A PLATYPUS AT ALL! HE'S AN ALIEN!

THAT METEORITE WAS HIS SPACE SHIP! THAT'S HOW HE GOT HERE!

WE'VE GOT TO DO SOMETHING!

EH, RIGHT! I KNOW JUST WHO TO CALL!

YOU DO?

YES! YOU...EH...JUST WAIT HERE! I'LL GET HELP!

SHORTLY...

ZOO

LOOKS LIKE IT'S UP TO ME TO SAVE LITTLE SOAPY! I JUST HOPE THE BUGS DON'T TURN UP FIRST!

PHEW! FINALLY! THE LAST ONE!

MY, UH...PLATYPUS! IS HE OKAY?

SURE! WHY WOULDN'T HE BE?

UM...NO REASON! BUT I NEED TO SEE HIM! PRONTO!

CALM DOWN, I'LL GO GET HIM! JUST WAIT HERE

LABORATORY

INSIDE THE LAB...

NOW STAY NICE AND STILL! IT WON'T HURT...MUCH!

WHAT THE BLAZES ARE YOU DOING?

DOING? I AM MAKING HISTORY BY INVESTIGATING A CREATURE HITHERTO UNKNOWN TO SCIENCE!

INTERSTELLAR *CURSES!* WE'RE CLOSE, BUT THE SCANNER HAS LOST OUR PREY!

NO MATTER! IF HE'S HERE, WE'LL FIND HIM!

LET'S TRY THIS WAY!

PHEW! A CLOSE SHAVE WITH A SHARP RAZOR!

I GOTTA TALK TO THE PEOPLE AT THE DUCKBURG SPACE CENTER, SOAPY! *THEY* SHOULD KNOW HOW TO HANDLE WILD ALIENS!

SOON...

HI! I NEED TO SEE THE DIRECTOR! IT'S *URGENT!*

SORRY, THAT'S IMPOSSIBLE! HE'S SUPERVISING A SPACE LAUNCH!

DUCKBURG SPACE CENTER

DIRECTOR! MY SCREEN'S GONE DOWN!

AND ALL OUR RADIO TRANSMITTERS ARE OUT!

ABORT THE LAUNCH!

EXCUSE ME!

HUH!?

I NEED TO TALK TO YOU ABOUT ALIENS!

ARE YOU NUTS? I'VE GOT A MAJOR EMERGENCY SITUATION HERE...

DIRECTOR!

THERE'S SOMETHING WEIRD ON THE SCREENS! FROM DEEP SPACE!

BLIP! BLIP!

IT'S ON COURSE FOR THE OUTSKIRTS OF DUCKBURG! IMPACT IN...ONE HOUR!

I DON'T KNOW WHAT THEIR GAME IS! BUT IF I KEEP MY WITS ABOUT ME, MAYBE I CAN GRAB SOAPY AND...

HUH!?

HEE! HEE! HEE!

SOAPY, AS YOU CALL HIM, IS *FINE*! HE'S TALKING TO HIS MOTHER RIGHT NOW!

HEE! HEE! SQUEAK!

BUT I THOUGHT YOU GUYS WERE HUNTING HIM... FOR *MONEY*!

...HE WAS A KIDNAP DROID SENT BY KRAG PIRATES WHO TRACKED THE DISTRESS SIGNAL OF SOAPY'S POD!

BY TRANSMITTING A FALSE RESCUE SIGNAL HE MEANT TO LURE SOAPY INTO A TRAP!

GASP!

BUT WHO ARE THE KRAG PIRATES? AND WHAT DO THEY WANT WITH LITTLE SOAPY? IS HE VALUABLE?

NO, BUT HE'S DANGEROUS! THE MOST DANGEROUS CREATURE IN OUR GALAXY!

OH C'MON! LITTLE SOAPY?

IT'S TRUE! ALL OF HIS SPECIES EMIT AN AURA THAT DISRUPTS UNPROTECTED MECHANICAL AND ELECTRICAL SYSTEMS!

BABIES ARE THE WORST! KRAGS USE THEM TO BLACKMAIL RICH HI-TECH PLANETS THAT OBVIOUSLY WOULDN'T WANT ONE SET LOOSE ON THEM!

THOUGH I HAVE TO ADMIT, I WON'T MISS HIS LUCK!

NOW FOR A LITTLE "POLICING" OF MY OWN!

AND SOON...

LOOKS LIKE HIS EXPERIMENTING DAYS ARE OVER!

YES! THANKS TO YOU!

BY THE WAY, WHAT HAPPENED TO THAT "ALIEN" OF YOURS?

LET'S JUST SAY HE'S BACK WHERE HE BELONGS, AND GLAD OF IT!

BOY! WHAT A DAY! NOW TO FIND THE KIDS AND EXPLAIN ABOUT SOAPY!

...AND SO I HANDED HIM OVER TO THE GALACTIC POLICE! HE WAS HAPPY TO BE GOING HOME, LET ME TELL YOU!

SIGH!

HE SURE WAS A CUTE LITTLE GUY!

GONNA MISS HIM!

GREETINGS, GOOD MAIL-RUNNERS! THIS FREEWHEELIN' MOUSE COULD SURE USE A *MUSHY SLUSHY!*

CERTAINLY, STRANGER. JUST A SEC'.

HEY, *YOU* HITTIN' THE ROAD TOO? WANNA *SPLIT* A SLUSHY?

NO, THANK YOU! I HAVE A *VERY IMPORTANT ASSIGNMENT*, MR. "FREEWHEELIN'." I'LL BE ON MY WAY NOW...

THAT'S A SHAME!

HERE YOU GO, STRANGER. ONE *TALL, COOL MUSHY SLUSHY.*

ON SECOND THOUGHT, FRIEND, MAKE IT A SIX-PACK *TO GO!*

"FREEWHEELIN'." *HMPH!* HOW *PRETENTIOUS!*

HEY, *MAIL-BABE!* HOWS ABOUT WE *CRUISE* OUT TO THE *BIG SAND* AND TOSS BACK A FEW MUSHY SLUSHIES TOGETHER? *WHADDYA SAY?*

I SAY, *NO THANK YOU!*

AW, *DON'T BE LIKE THAT!* WE'LL WATCH THE SUN SET. IT'LL BE *ROMANTIC!*

I'M SURE IT WILL. *ENJOY!*

SOME OF US DON'T HAVE TIME FOR SUCH *FRIVOLITY.* MY WORK IS *PRETTY DARN IMPORTANT,* MR. "FREEWHEELIN'!"

I'LL BET. DELIVERING BILLS AND CATALOGS. AND THE NAME'S *MICKEY-MICKEY MOUSE.*

OH, WELL, CAN'T WIN 'EM ALL! TOO BAD, THOUGH. SHE *WAS* FIESTY!

WONDER WHAT WAS SO IMPORTANT ABOUT THAT PACKAGE SHE WAS HUGGING?

NOTHING CAN STOP THEM... WELL, ALMOST NOTHING...

WAIT UP, *MAIL-GAL!* I GOT SOMETHIN' FOR YA!

THAT WOULD BE ME, *PETE, SPECIAL DELIVERY!* HAW!

RROOAR

M-MY *BIKE!*

YOU CALL THIS *PARKING!?*

AH...I SEE THE *NIGHTMARE* ISN'T OVER...

LOOK, I'M *SORRY* ABOUT YOUR MOTORCYCLE, BUT SOME *LUNATIC* JUST *CUT OFF* MY *MAILVAN!*

LIKELY STORY! I'VE SEEN *WOMEN DRIVERS* BEFORE!

HAH! BY WRECKING *YOUR* BIKE, I BET I JUST MADE OUR ROADS *A LITTLE SAFER!*

REACH FOR THE SKY, RUNTS! I'VE COME TO *COLLECT MY MAIL...*

AND I **AIN'T** THE KIND OF GUY TO SIT WAITIN' BY HIS MAILBOX!

A FEW SORRY MINUTES LATER...

I'LL HAVE YOU KNOW THAT **ROBBING** A MAIL-RUNNER IS A **SERIOUS OFFENSE!**

OOH, I'M **SHAKIN'** IN MY **BOOTIES!**

TIGHT ENOUGH FOR YA, **MOUSE?** HAW, HAW!

♪ **I'M OUTTA JAIL AN' I'M FREE! AND I GOT MY SPECIAL DELIVERY! AND IT AIN'T EVEN MY BIRTHDAY-HEE HEE!** ♪

WHY DON'T YOU **DO** SOMETHING, **TOUGH GUY!**

IN CASE YOU HAVEN'T NOTICED, I'M **ALL TIED UP!**

TIME TO **UNWRAP** YOU!

CAN'T *WAIT* TA SEE WHAT'S INSIDE! OOH, BUT I LOVE *GUESSING GAMES*, TOO!

HMM, SOMETHIN' *SOLID*...AND A *LI'L HEAVY* FOR ITS SIZE...

KLUNKITY-KLUNK

I BET IT'S THE *WORLD'S BIGGEST RUBY!* OR *EMERALD!* OR *DIAMOND!*

ENOUGH WITH THE GLOATING! *OPEN IT* ALREADY!

HAW, HAW! YOU DON'T GET IT, DO YA?

GLOATING IS IN THE BAD GUY'S *JOB DESCRIPTION!* THAT, AND PINCHING THE *SCHNOZZ* OF *PIPSQUEAKS* LIKE YOU!

SO *PUNY* AN' *HELPLESS!* AWW...

HAR! NOTHIN' BEATS BULLYING A *WEAKLING!* GETTIN' THE LOOT IS JUST *ICIN' ON THE CAKE!*

YOU'RE FORGETTING THAT THE *GOOD* GUYS AND GALS *ALWAYS* WIN!

ONLY IN THE *COMIC BOOKS,* SWEETS.

NOW TA GET WHAT'S *COMIN'* TA ME!

WHAZZAT? YOU AIN'T TRYIN' SOMETHIN' *FUNNY*, ARE YA, RUNT?

SNAP

ATTACKIN' FROM BEHIND? AIN'T THAT AGAINST THE *GOOD GUY RULES?*

NOPE! NOT EVEN IN THE *COMIC BOOKS!*

KRACK

AND SO...

TIGHT ENOUGH FOR YA, *BIG* SQUEAK?

I'M SURE YOU WON'T MIND IF WE BORROW...

"...YOUR VEHICLE!"

WE'LL DELIVER THIS PACKAGE *LONG BEFORE* HE GETS LOOSE FROM *THOSE* KNOTS!

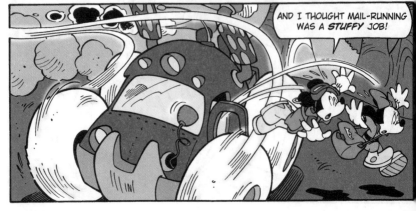

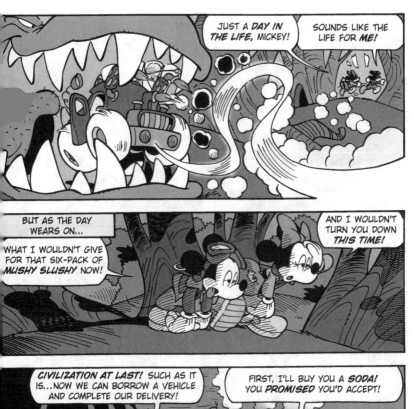

MEANWHILE... THIS IS JUST A SETBACK! THAT PACKAGE IS *MINE!*

SOME COUNTRY BUMPKIN'S BOUND TO COME BY AND...*WELL, THAR SHE BLOWS!*

...SO YOU *ACCIDENTALLY TIED YOURSELF UP,* HUH? GAWRSH! THAT TAKES *TALENT!* WELL, HILLBILLY GOOF TO THE RESCUE!

THANK YOU, KIND SIR!

AN' HERE'S YOUR *REWARD!*

A BIKE, *AND A PERSUADER!* I'M BACK IN THE BAD-GUY BIZ! HAW!

EARLY NEXT MORNING...

IT WAS A PLEASURE TO HAVE YOU FOLKS DROP BY. WE DON'T GET VISITORS MUCH 'ROUND THESE PARTS....

I WISH WE COULD STAY LONGER. THANKS FOR EVERYTHING, JERONIMUS.

WHAT'S WITH THE *BALLOON*, JERONIMUS?

OH, JUST ANOTHER *SILLY INVENTION* OF MINE THAT DIDN'T PAN OUT. IT'S YOURS IF YOU WANT IT.

IT TOOK *ALL NIGHT* TO GET HERE, BUT IT LOOKS LIKE IT'LL BE WORTH IT!

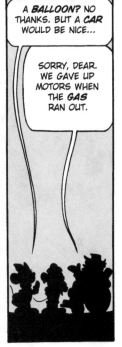

A *BALLOON?* NO THANKS. BUT A *CAR* WOULD BE NICE...

SORRY, DEAR. WE GAVE UP MOTORS WHEN THE *GAS* RAN OUT.

HE'S **HEADING** FOR THE **GATE!**

STOP THAT SCOUNDREL! **HURRY!**

THE WIND'S BLOWING THE RIGHT WAY!

WE'LL **NEVER** CATCH UP!

WE'VE GOT A BREEZE, BUT WE NEED A **HURRICANE!**

OOH, I'M SO **SCARED** OF THE **FLYING SQUIRRELS!**

WHAT *LUCK!* WE'RE DRIFTING TOWARD *RUFFNECK ROCK!*

CAN'T WAIT TO SEE WHAT'S *IN* THIS PACKAGE!

TIME TO BREAK OUT THAT HILLBILLY'S....

...*PERSUADER!*

JUST THE THING FER PICKIN' OFF *SQUIRRELS!*

BLAMM

WE'RE SO HIGH UP I'M GETTING A NOSEBLEED!

MANY "RIGHT WAYS" LATER...

MAYBE OUR LUCK'S RUN OUT...

NO IT HASN'T! PETE WILL NEVER BE ABLE TO TRACK US NOW! AND LOOK, THERE'S THE SIGN!

RUFFNECK ROCK

WE'RE ALMOST THERE. WE JUST NEED TO FIND THE MAILBOX.

AND THEN WE'LL FINALLY FIND OUT WHAT'S IN THIS DARN PACKAGE!

THAT'LL BE SOME KIND OF REWARD, AT LEAST.

A JOB WELL DONE IS A REWARD IN ITS OWN RIGHT!

THAT'S STRANGE. NO HOUSE. JUST A STEEL DOOR IN THE MOUNTAINSIDE.

WHAT A WEIRD PLACE TO LIVE!

MAYBE IT'S AN OFFICE OR SOMETHING. ANYWAY, HERE'S THE *MAILBOX.*

DARN! NOW WE'LL *NEVER* FIND OUT WHAT'S INSIDE!

HEY, MINNIE...WHAT IF PETE SHOWS UP *BEFORE* THIS MR. ANONYMOUSE CHECKS HIS MAILBOX?

LET IT *GO*, MICKEY!

OH, ALL RIGHT. I'LL RING THE BELL AND *WARN HIM* TO TAKE IT INSIDE.

AND TO *OPEN IT* RIGHT AWAY!

WHAT CAN I DO FOR YOU?

DESTROYING THE CITIES WAS JUST THE *FIRST STEP!* WITH MY *HULKERBOT* I SHALL ESTABLISH MY *RULE OVER ALL!*

THE DOOR *CLOSED!* WE'RE *TRAPPED* WITH THIS *NUT!*

WE SHOULD'VE LET *PETE* HAVE THAT PACKAGE AFTER ALL.

SPEAKING OF PETE...

DARN! LOST THE *PACKAGE RATS'* TRAIL! I'LL JUST HAVE TO *INTERCEPT* THEM *BEFORE* THEY DELIVER THAT PARCEL!

AT LAST THE WORLD WILL BE *FORCED* TO *APPRECIATE* MY *GENIUS!* THE HULKERBOT MAKES ME *INVINCIBLE!* NO ONE WILL BE ABLE TO *STAND AGAINST ME!*

IN MY EXPERIENCE, THE *BIGGER* THE BADDIES, THE MORE THEY *BOAST,* AND THE *LESS* THEY...

AND SO... **NOW** CAN WE OPEN THAT PACKAGE, MINNIE?

I **SUPPOSE** SO...

HUH? **KETCHUP?!**

SPARE **FUEL** FOR THE HULKERBOT'S SPECIALIZED **ENGINE!** IT'S **RARE STUFF** NOW, AND I WANTED TO BE SURE I HAD A **REFILL** BEFORE I SET OUT!

WHAT ABOUT **ME?!** ALL THIS **WORK** FOR A **MEASLY** BOTTLE OF **KETCHUP!** AND NOT EVEN A BURGER TO PUT IT ON...**BAW!**

YOU EVIL TYPES AIM **TOO HIGH!** ALL **I** NEED TO BE HAPPY IS A **SIX PACK OF MUSHY SLUSHY** AND A **GREAT GAL** TO SHARE 'EM WITH!

MORE DISNEY excitement TO COME!

If you like this comic, you'll want to be on board for all the fun in the months to come, with Gemstone Publishing's exciting line of Disney comic books.

For collectors: Walt Disney's Comics and Stories and Uncle Scrooge, providing the best of vintage and recent classic tales by such highly-acclaimed creators as Carl Barks, Pat Block, Daniel Branca, Cesar Ferioli, David Gerstein, Michael T. Gilbert, Daan Jippes, Don Markstein, Pat McGreal, Dave Rawson, Don Rosa, Noel Van Horn, William Van Horn, and many more. These books are 64 pages and in the sturdy, squarebound prestige format that collectors love.

©2003 Disney Enterprises, Inc.

For readers on the go: Donald Duck Adventures, the first title in our new 5" X 7½" "Take-Along Comic" series, gives you long adventure stories starring Mickey, Donald, Scrooge, and others in modern stories that take them beyond the limits of space and time.

For readers of all ages: Donald Duck and Mickey Mouse and Friends, offering Disney fans the best contemporary Mouse and Duck stories in the familiar 32-page, stapled, comic book format.

Look for them at your local comic shop! Can't find a comic shop? Try the Toll Free Comic Shop Locator Service at (888) COMIC BOOK for the shop nearest you! If you can't find Gemstone's Disney comics in your neighborhood you may subscribe at no extra charge, and we'll pay the postage! Use the coupon below, or a copy:

Mail this coupon to: Gemstone Publishing, P.O. Box 469, West Plains, Missouri 65775.

☐ Walt Disney's Comics and Stories: $83.40 for 12 issues ($90.00 Canada, payable in US funds)
☐ Walt Disney's Uncle Scrooge: $83.40 for 12 issues ($90.00 Canada, payable in US funds)
☐ Walt Disney's Donald Duck: $35.40 for 12 issues ($40.00 Canada, payable in US funds)
☐ Walt Disney's Mickey Mouse and Friends: $35.40 for 12 issues ($40.00 Canada, payable in US funds)
☐ D.D.A.: $95.40 for 12 issues ($105.00 Canada, payable in US funds)

Name: _____
Address: _____
City: _____ State: _____ Zip Code: _____
Email: _____
☐ Visa ☐ MasterCard ☐ Other   Card # _____ Exp. Date: _____

GEMSTONE PUBLISHING

www.gemstonepub.com

THIS DINKY COIN FIVE DOLLARS?! OH, I SEE - IT'S GOLD!

EVERYTHING IN YOUR MONEY BIN IS GOLD NOW, UNCLE SCROOGE! WHAT GIVES?

A FURTHER FORTUNE IN THE MAKING! THE PRICE OF GOLD HAS PLUMMETED TO ITS LOWEST POINT IN DECADES!

SO I'VE CONVERTED ALL MY WEALTH TO GOLD - STOCKS, BONDS, BILLS, COINS - THE LOT!

WHY?! IF NOBODY WANTS GOLD NOW...

I KNOW THAT THE PRICE WILL SOON CLIMB AGAIN! THEN I CONVERT MY HOLDINGS BACK AND MAKE A PROFIT!

ONE PERSON'S JUNK IS ANOTHER PERSON'S TREASURE!

IT'S A LESSON FEW BUT I TAKE TO HEART! A LESSON I'VE SPENT MY LIFE EXPLOITING!

AND THAT'S WHAT SEPARATES ME FROM YOU, KNUCKLEHEAD!

HUH?!

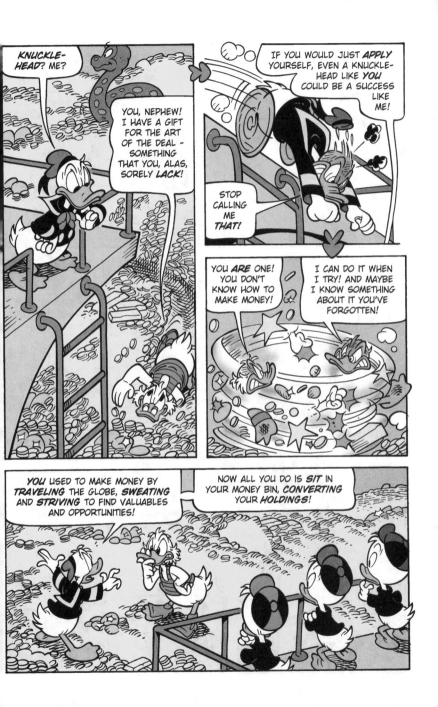

SHORTLY...

COME ON, UNCA DONALD! BUY SOMETHING FOR *CHARITY!*

SNORT! IT ALL LOOKS LIKE *JUNK* TO ME! MAYBE I'LL JUST *HOLD ONTO* THAT FIVE-DOLLAR COIN!

DUCKBURG DAY SCHOOL'S ANNUAL RUMMAGE SALE

AND WASTE AN OPPORTUNITY TO *TURN JUNK* INTO *TREASURE?*

BUT *SOME* JUNK ISN'T *WORTH* THE EFFORT!

GRIPE! I'LL TAKE THIS *BRICK* FOR TWO BITS! MAYBE I CAN USE IT FOR A *PAPERWEIGHT* OR A *DOORSTOP!*

GASP! A *GOLD* COIN!

SAY! IT LOOKS *REALLY* OLD! AND THERE'S AN *INSCRIPTION* CARVED ON IT! WONDER IF IT'S AN *ANTIQUE?*

WHERE ARE YOU GOING, UNCA DONALD?

TO *FIND OUT!* MAYBE IT'S MY CHANCE TO PROVE MY POINT TO UNCLE SCROOGE!

IT TURNS *IRON INTO GOLD!* THESE MARKINGS ARE A SUMILTIAN *INCANTATION!*

WHEN UNCLE SCROOGE GETS COMPLACENT, DONALD DUCK BEATS HIM TO A *REAL TREASURE!*

OH, BROTHER!

WATCH! I'LL POINT THE STONE AT THIS IRON FIGURINE AND MUTTER THE MUMBO-JUMBO...

ALSOBLOM MUICHILTO KULUSHI!

NOTHING *HAPPENED,* UNCA DONALD!

AWP! I MUST'VE GOTTEN SOMETHING WRONG!

I'LL JUST CHECK MY PRONOUNCIATION WITH THE BOOKS! HUFF! HURF! THIS STONE *MUST* WORK! IT JUST *HAS* TO WORK! JIBBER! SQUEAK!

UH-OH!

UNCA DONALD'S *TOO ANXIOUS* TO TEACH UNCLE SCROOGE A LESSON!

HE'S HEADED FOR A *LETDOWN!* UNLESS...

TOO *LATE!* HE'S HALFWAY THERE ALREADY!

OH, WELL! NO LASTING HARM DONE, I SUPPOSE...

SO A KNUCKLEHEAD LIKE ME CAN'T *PROVE* THAT YOU'RE SET IN YOUR WAYS, HUH?

GET IT OVER WITH, NEPHEW!

WHILE YOU SIT AROUND CONVERTING YOUR HOLDINGS, *I* FIND *REAL* VALUABLES!

WATCH THAT *IRON* FIGURINE, UNCLE SCROOGE - *ALSOBLOM MUCHILTO KULUSHI!*

HUH? WHAT'S GOING ON? THIS...THIS STONE'S SUPPOSED TO TURN IRON TO *GOLD!*

LOOKS LIKE YOU GOT *TOOK*, DONALD!

NOW, IF YOU'RE DONE FOOLING AROUND, I'M OFF TO THE BIN TO TAKE MY AFTERNOON SWIM!

WAIT, UNCLE SCROOGE! I- I- I THINK IT TAKES A LITTLE *WHILE* TO WORK!

I DON'T *GET* IT! WHY-

YIMINY YIKES!

YAAARRGH!!!

MY GOLD!! IT'S ALL BEEN CHANGED TO *IRON!!* YOU KNUCKLE-HEAD, *YOU* DID THIS SOMEHOW, I *KNOW* IT!

IT WAS MY *STONE!* THAT'S GOTTA BE IT!

STAY C-C-*CALM*, UNCLE SCROOGE! WE'LL FIND *SOMEONE* WHO CAN TELL US WHAT WENT WRONG!

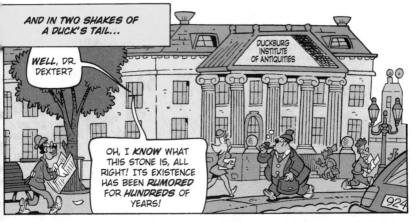

AND IN TWO SHAKES OF A DUCK'S TAIL...

WELL, DR. DEXTER?

DUCKBURG INSTITUTE OF ANTIQUITIES

OH, I *KNOW* WHAT THIS STONE IS, ALL RIGHT! ITS EXISTENCE HAS BEEN *RUMORED* FOR *HUNDREDS* OF YEARS!

I ALWAYS THOUGHT THE RUMORS WERE A *JOKE!* HEH! AND NOW HERE IT *IS!* THAT'S FUNNY!

IT'S NO LAUGHING MATTER! WHERE DID THAT INFERNAL BRICK *COME* FROM?!

THE LEGENDS SAY IT WAS MADE BY AN ANCIENT *ALCHEMIST* NAMED *KNICKODEMOS*, WHO SPENT HIS LIFE TRYING TO TURN *IRON* INTO *GOLD!* HAR!

"IT SEEMS OLD KNICK WAS A VERY POOR ALCHEMIST - IN BOTH SENSES OF THE WORD! HE OWNED ONLY ONE GOLD COIN TO EXPERIMENT ON!"

"AFTER YEARS OF STRUGGLING, HE WAS STILL UNSUC-CESSFUL!"

KNUCKLEHEAD KNICKO-DEMOS, THEY CALLED HIM! HE HAD NOTHING UPSTAIRS BUT A FEW MOTHS!

WHAT YOU HAVE HERE, MY FRIEND, IS THE *KNUCKLE-HEAD STONE!*

GROAN!

WHAT ABOUT KNICKO-DEMOS?

"OH, HE EMBARKED ON A QUEST TO FIND A MYTHIC LOST VALLEY OF GOLD - IN A FAR-OFF LAND ACROSS THE SEA WHERE THE SUN RISES!"

"I GUESS HE THOUGHT IF HE COULD CHANGE SOME OF THAT GOLD TO IRON, IT WOULD PROVE HIS DISCOVERY TO OTHERS!"

"BUT HIS JOURNEY CARRIED HIM RIGHT OFF THE OLD MAPS! HE WAS NEVER HEARD FROM AGAIN!"

AS FOR THE VALLEY? HUMPH! WE SCIENTISTS DOUBT *IT* EVER EXISTED!

BUT WHAT ABOUT THE *MARKINGS* ON THE *STONE?*

THEY *CLEARLY* SAY *"IRON INTO GOLD"*! A DIRECT *PATH* LEADS FROM THE LUMP OF LEAD THROUGH THE MAGIC SYMBOL TO THE GOLD COINS!

HO-HO! I CAN *SEE* HOW *YOU* MIGHT HAVE MISUNDERSTOOD THAT! SEE, WE READ ANCIENT SUMILTIAN *RIGHT TO LEFT*!

GET IT?! SNICKER! START WITH GOLD, THE MAGIC INCANTATION IS GIVEN AND - *VOILA* - *IRON*!

AND THE MOST HILARIOUS PART IS... *OHOHEEHEEHAHA!!* THERE'S NO WAY TO *REVERSE* THE PROCESS!

GRRRRRR!

GURK!

DON'T WASTE YOUR ENERGY, UNCLE SCROOGE! YOU'VE GOT SOME SERIOUS *THINKING* TO DO!

MANY PHONE CALLS LATER...

CUSHLAMACREE! WORD IS SPREADING LIKE *WILDFIRE* ABOUT MY MONEY PROBLEMS! *EMPLOYEES* ARE *DESERTING* MY FINANCIAL EMPIRE LIKE RATS FLEEING A SINKING SHIP!

MY BUSINESS CONCERNS HAVE BEEN BROUGHT TO A *STANDSTILL!* HOW COULD THINGS GET ANY *WORSE?!*

BRRR-RIIINNNG!

WHAT?!

THIS IS A FRIENDLY REMINDER THAT YOUR *PROPERTY TAXES* ARE DUE BY *SIX O' CLOCK* TONIGHT!

IF THEY ARE NOT *PAID* BY THEN, WE'LL *FORECLOSE* ON YOUR *HOME* AND ALL YOUR *PROPERTIES!*

LISTEN, YOU! I'VE HAD *ENOUGH* –

THIS IS A *RECORDING!* HAVE A NICE *DAY!* CLICK!

LATER THAT NIGHT...

KEEP LOOKING, BOYS! WITH UNCLE SCROOGE *SHUT OUT* OF HIS HOUSE AND MONEY BIN, THERE'S NO *TELLING* WHERE HE'LL GO!

OVER HERE! I THINK I'VE FOUND HIM!

SLEEPING ON A PARK BENCH! ALL WRAPPED UP IN *NEWSPAPERS* TO KEEP WARM!

WHAT A SORRY SIGHT!

YOU *CAN'T* SPEND THE NIGHT HERE, UNCLE SCROOGE!

LEAVE ME BE, NEPHEW! I'M A *PAUPER* NOW! THIS SUITS MY NEW STATION IN LIFE!

GOSH! I'VE NEVER SEEN HIM LIKE THIS!

I *REFUSE* TO BE A BURDEN!

WELL, YOU'RE STAYING AT OUR PLACE ANYWAY! I *INSIST!*

SHORTLY ...

POOR UNCA SCROOGE! HE FEELS LOWER THAN A LIMBO DANCER WHOSE KNEES JUST GAVE OUT!

WE'D LIKE TO *HELP* HIM, BUT... *WHAT* CAN WE DO?

I KNOW! *I'LL* GET A *JOB!*

HUH?!

TO MAKE UP FOR MY *BLUNDER,* EVERYTHING I EARN WILL BE *YOURS!*

DONALD, I'M TOUCHED THAT YOU'D CONSIDER SOMETHING SO FUNDAMENTALLY OPPOSED TO YOUR BASIC NATURE, BUT...

WE KIDS WILL PITCH IN, TOO! WE CAN GET A *PAPER ROUTE!*

AND I HEAR THEY'RE LOOKING FOR A *NIGHT WATCHMAN* AT KOOGLE'S DEPARTMENT STORE! *THAT'S* SOMETHING I BET *YOU* COULD HANDLE, UNCLE SCROOGE!

YOU'LL BE BACK ON YOUR FEET IN *NO* TIME!

SIGH! YOU CAN'T AMASS WEALTH LIKE *I* HAD THROUGH COMMON *WAGE LABOR!*

WHY, TO GET *MY* FORTUNE ROLLING IN THE FIRST PLACE, *I* HAD TO *TRAVEL* TO THE KLONDIKE! I HAD TO *STAKE* A *CLAIM!*

THEN, ONCE I HAD A STRIKE, I HAD TO *COAX* AND *NURTURE* EACH DIME TO *GROW* AND *MULTIPLY!*

AND TO THINK...IT ALL STARTED WITH *THIS!* MY NUMBER ONE DIME!

WAIT A MINUTE! GOOD OLD NUMBER ONE!

A REMINDER THAT *ANYTHING* CAN BE ACCOMPLISHED IF YOU *ROLL UP YOUR SLEEVES* AND *WORK* FOR IT!

DONALD, I *DID* LET MYSELF GET *COMPLACENT* AND *LAZY!* *LOUNGING* IN MY MONEY BIN! *PLAYING* WITH THE PRICE OF GOLD! *PAH!*

WELL, BY GUM, I CAN *START FROM SCRATCH!*

THERE'S A *FORTUNE* TO BE MADE! EVEN IF IT TAKES *ANOTHER LIFETIME!*

"...TO KEEP MY BIG MOUTH SHUT!"

MY THEORY IS THAT THE LAND ACROSS THE OCEAN FROM ANCIENT SUMILTIA MUST BE PRESENT-DAY PORTO GORDO!

ITS VAST, UNEXPLORED JUNGLES WOULD EXPLAIN WHY THE VALLEY HAS NEVER BEEN DISCOVERED!

AND *THAT'S* WHERE THIS TRAMP STEAMER IS BOUND FOR?! BUT HOW WILL WE *PAY* FOR THE TRIP?

BARGES

BAILS

THE CAPTAIN IS AN OLD FRIEND OF MINE! HE'LL LET US *WORK* FOR OUR PASSAGE!

WORK?!

CERTAINLY! *I'LL* BE A *COOK*, AND *YOU'LL* BE *SWABBING DECKS!*

AWP!

FULL STEAM AHEAD...

AH! THE OPEN SEA *INVIGORATES* ME! I'M MORE *ALIVE* THAN I'VE BEEN IN AGES!

AMAZINGLY, DUE TO MY KNUCKLEHEAD NEPHEW *FOULING UP!*

DONALD, MY LAD, YOU'VE GIVEN ME BACK A *TREASURE* I *FORGOT* I HAD!

YEAH, THAT'S SWELL...

...BUT THE OPEN SEA'S GOT *ME* FEELING A MITE *QUEASY!*

WHAT'S THIS LOLLYGAGGING? I'LL HAVE NO *LAYABOUTS* ON *MY* SHIP! YOU CALL *THIS* A CLEAN DECK?!

UURRRP!

SWAB THE WHOLE THING *AGAIN!*

...AYE-AYE, SIR...

GRRRR! I'D *NEVER* HAVE WOUND UP IN SUCH A MISERABLE SITUATION IF IT WASN'T FOR KNICKODEMO'S DRAT-FRATTED *KNUCKLEHEAD STONE!*

TOSS!

WELL, I'VE *HAD* IT WITH THIS MENACE OF A BRICK! TIME TO *DEEP-SIX* IT!

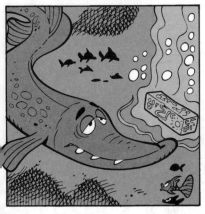

YUM!

THERE! THE THING'S AT THE *BOTTOM* OF THE OCEAN! IT WON'T CAUSE ANY TROUBLE *THERE!*

MAGOG

ONE WEEK LATER...

AT LAST! SCENIC PORTO GORDO! THIS IS WHERE OUR QUEST TRULY *BEGINS*, DONALD!

FINALLY! I COULDN'T SCRUB ANOTHER DECK! EVEN MY *BLISTERS* HAVE BLISTERS!

SCROOGE, YOUR MEALS WERE A *TREAT* FOR THE TASTEBUDS! I'D LIKE TO REWARD YOU WITH A *BONUS*!

BELIEVE IT OR NOT, MY FRIEND, I'M NOT *INTERESTED* IN *CASH*! BUT I WOULDN'T SAY NO TO THAT *ROWBOAT* THERE!

DONE!

HEY! WHAT ABOUT *ME*? WHAT DO *I* GET FOR ALL THE EXEMPLARY *MOPPING* I DID?!

SHOULDA SEEN *THAT* COMING!

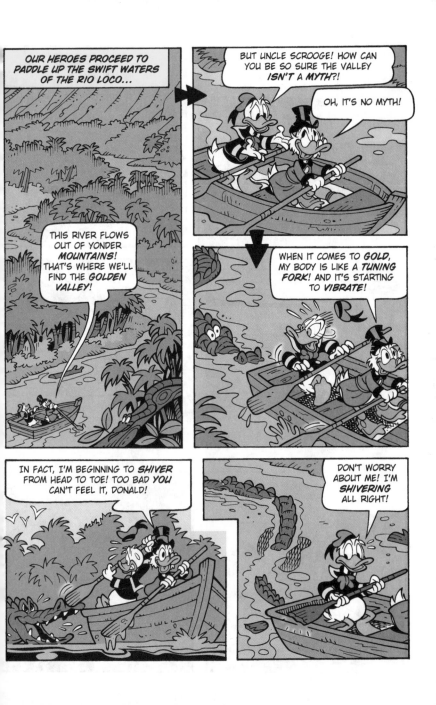

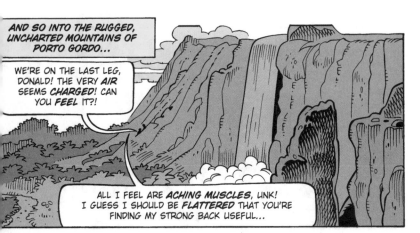

AND SO INTO THE RUGGED, UNCHARTED MOUNTAINS OF PORTO GORDO...

WE'RE ON THE LAST LEG, DONALD! THE VERY *AIR* SEEMS *CHARGED!* CAN YOU *FEEL* IT?!

ALL I FEEL ARE *ACHING MUSCLES*, UNK! I GUESS I SHOULD BE *FLATTERED* THAT YOU'RE FINDING MY STRONG BACK USEFUL...

...BUT I'M AT A *LOSS* AS TO WHY WE NEED THIS SHIFTLESS, BRAYING *BAGGAGE!*

HEEE-HAAW!

ALL IN GOOD TIME, NEPHEW!

RIGHT NOW I'M *REVELING* IN THE *EUPHORIA* OF IMPENDING PROSPECTS, AS I FELT WHEN I ARRIVED IN THE KLONDIKE! I AM *YOUNG* ONCE MORE!

THE ENTIRE *FABRIC* OF MY BEING SHOUTS THAT OUR *GOAL* IS IMMINENT! WE'LL STOP AND CAMP HERE FOR THE NIGHT!

PANT! SUITS *ME!* WHEEZE!

TSK! THE *IRONY* IS, OLD KNICK OBVIOUSLY *NEVER* MADE IT HERE WITH HIS *STONE!*

HOW DO YOU *KNOW* HE DIDN'T?

LOOK AROUND! IF HE *HAD,* THESE WOULD BE MOUNTAINS OF *IRON!* BAD LUCK FOR HIM, GOOD LUCK FOR ME!

HMM! THE VILLAGES HERE HAVE BEEN *ISOLATED* FROM THE REST OF THE WORLD FOR TIME OUT OF MIND! HOPE MY *SIGN LANGUAGE* SKILLS AREN'T TOO RUSTY!

THAT BIG DRINK OF WATER MUST BE THE LOCAL CHIEF!

SIR, I AM *MCDUCK!* I'VE COME TO STRIKE A *DEAL* FOR ONE TINY VEIN OF *GOLD* AT THE FAR END OF YOUR VALLEY!

IN RETURN FOR THAT, I'LL GIVE YOU THIS *PURE SILK* HAT, SLIGHTLY USED!

HE'S TAKING IT! LOOKS LIKE YOU'VE GOT A *DEAL!*

SHORTLY...

SO *THIS* IS WHERE YOU BEGIN TO BUILD YOUR FORTUNE AGAIN, EH? OKAY! WHERE DO WE START?

RELAX, DONALD! YOU'VE DONE *YOUR* PART! IT'S UP TO *ME* AND ME ALONE TO MINE THIS CLAIM!

SCROOGE DIGS! HE BURROWS...

...HE SWEATS AND SLAVES...

...FINDING JOY IN THE REWARDS OF HARD WORK! FEELING FULFILLMENT IN HIS ACCOMPLISHMENTS...

AND DONALD? WELL...DONALD DOES JUST AS HE'S TOLD...

WEEKS PASS! AND AT LAST...

THERE! I'LL ONLY TAKE AS MUCH GOLD AS THIS LITTLE BURRO CAN PACK OUT!

WAKE UP, NEPHEW! TIME TO *GO!*

ZZZZ- *HUH?!* SO *SOON?!* I WAS IN THE MIDDLE OF A SWEET *DREAM!*

SO LONG, CHIEF CHOMA! THANKS FOR YOUR GENEROUS *HOSPITALITY!* I'M OFF TO PARLAY THIS MODEST AMOUNT OF GOLD INTO A *GREATER* FORTUNE!

I'LL CONVERT IT TO CASH AND WORK UP FROM THERE, JUST AS I DID WITH MY NUMBER ONE DIME! DID I EVER SHOW YOU OLD NUMBER ONE, CHIEF?

IT'S RIGHT HERE IN MY POC-

WHOOPS! I FORGOT I WAS STILL CARRYING THAT *FIGURINE!*

?!!!

AND SO ...

ALL'S WELL THAT *ENDS* WELL, LADS! MY MONEY BIN'S FILLED WITH *GOLD* ONCE MORE!

CHIEF CHOMA AND HIS TRIBE WILL RECEIVE THE LAST SHIPMENT OF IRON TODAY! THEY'RE QUITE *PLEASED* WITH THE TRADE THEY MADE!

THE CHIEF'S A MAN AFTER MY OWN HEART! HIS PEOPLE HAVE PLENTY OF GOLD LEFT - AND HE'S *CORNERED* THE MARKET FOR *IRON* IN THE AREA!

EVERY *OTHER* TRIBE WITHIN A *HUNDRED-MILE RADIUS* WANTS TO *TRADE* WITH HIM TO GET SOME OF IT!

STRANGE, ISN'T IT?

WHAT'S STRANGE, UNCA DONALD?

HOW *WE* VALUE *GOLD* BECAUSE OF ITS *COLOR* AND *TEXTURE* AND THE *RARITY* OF IT...

...AND CHIEF CHOMA'S PEOPLE VALUE *IRON* FOR THE EXACT *SAME* REASONS!

WELL, IT'S LIKE UNCA SCROOGE SAID A FEW WEEKS AGO...

AND AS I'VE *LIVED* SINCE... *ONE PERSON'S JUNK...*

...IS ANOTHER *PERSON'S TREASURE!*

HMM! YEAH, SURE! BUT I STILL WISH I'D NEVER *FOUND* THAT KNUCKLEHEAD STONE!

Comic Characters Delivered Weekly

When you log onto

SCOOP

Scoop is the FREE, weekly, e-newsletter from Gemstone Publishing and Diamond International Galleries for collectors and pop culture enthusiasts of all ages. It covers the past, present and future of comic character collectibles, the latest industry news, media happenings and so much more - to get you tuned into those trends that have shaped our history and our development as a society. Read the latest about the characters you love - and get to know other characters both old and new. So don't wait - visit **http://scoop.diamondgalleries.com** to check it all out!

All characters ™ & © 2003 their respective trademark and copyright holders. All rights reserved.